MINISTER'S LITTLE INSTRUCTION BOOK

Timeless Wisdom and Practical
Advice for Ministers and Lay Leaders

by
Dr. Stan Toler

Tulsa, Oklahoma

Minister's Little Instruction Book —
Timeless Wisdom and Practical
Advice for Ministers and Lay Leaders
ISBN 1-56292-087-1
Copyright © 1994 by Dr. Stan Toler

Published by Honor Books
P. O. Box 55388
Tulsa, Oklahoma 74155

• Introduction •

The *Minister's Little Instruction Book* is a reflection of the many lessons I have learned in my twenty-five-plus years in the ministry. It also includes inspirational quotes and humor that have been encouraging to me at the lowest points in my ministerial journey.

There have been four great influences in my life and ministry. They are John Maxwell, Tom Hermiz, Terry Toler, and Melvin Maxwell. Many of the statements in this book are gleaned from the insights I have recalled from them.

It is my prayer that this book will bring a smile to your face, a challenge to your mind and encouragement on your spiritual journey.

Stan Toler
Ephesians 3:20-21

Dedicated to some of the finest Christian laymen that I know. . .

Jim Van Hook, Jack Hollingsworth, Barney Hall, Buddy Vaughan, Melvin Hatley, O. A. Garr III, Jim Hatton and Jim Hendershot.

Special thanks to Derl G. Keefer, Wes Williams, Beth Trees, Dale Mathews, Dean Diehl and Gina Smith for their time and effort in making this project possible.

1 · A good life is the best sermon.

2 · The role of a preacher is to comfort the afflicted and afflict the comfortable.

3 · Don't get caught up in the numbers game.

ৡৡৡ

4 · Behold the turtle. It makes progress only when it sticks its neck out.

ৡৡৡ

5 · Never go to the restroom with your lavaliere mic on!

6 · For every loser there is a winner. You simply have to make up your mind which you want to be.

7 · Life is not so much a matter of position as of disposition.

❧❧❧

8 · If you must counsel,
counsel the opposite sex
with the office door open!

❧❧❧

9 • Celebrate a major victory with your congregation.

10 • "Record" your ideas on a tape recorder in order to play back at your leisure.

(11) • Feed your faith and doubt will starve to death.

૪ૐ૪ૐ૪ૐ

12 · Join the local PTA.

૪ૐ૪ૐ૪ૐ

13· Don't seek honors which come from men. The pastor stands or falls before God and not men.
– *W. A. Criswell*

14· The law of church committees: "If you leave the room, you're elected."

15· Of all the things you can wear, your expression is the most important.

16 · Keep your words soft
and sweet. You never
know when you're going
to have to eat them.

17 · Procrastination is the thief of time.

18 · Have a vision-planning retreat.

19 · One thing you can give and still keep is your word.

20 · Carry only the key
to *your* office.

21 · Be like a postage stamp — stick to one thing till you get there.

22 · Call your parishioners on their anniversaries and birthdays.

23 · "People seldom improve when they have no other model but themselves to copy after."
— *Goldsmith*

ନ୍ଧ ନ୍ଧ ନ୍ଧ

24 · Underspend the church budget!

ନ୍ଧ ନ୍ଧ ନ୍ଧ

25 · Always get three bids!

26 · Creativity has been built into every one of us; it's part of our design. – *Ted Engstrom*

27 · Get an annual physical check-up.

❧❧❧

28 · Keep your car clean!

❧❧❧

29 · There can be no rainbow without a cloud and a storm.

30 · Give more than 10%.

31 · Let others make announcements and lead the services; otherwise you'll die from overexposure.

32 · Preach the Word!

33 · To keep extra weight off — never eat after 6 p.m.!

34 · At age 20, we worry about what others think of us. At 40, we don't care what they think of us. At 60, we discover they haven't been thinking about us at all. – *Mike Duduit*

ଈଈଈ

(35)· Take your spouse out to
dinner on a regular basis.

ଈଈଈ

36 • Learn to be a coach . . . empower your church leaders to act!

37 • Delegate! Delegate! Delegate!

38 • If you can laugh at it, then you can live with it.

ॐ ॐ ॐ

39 · You don't have to have
three P's and a pun to
be a good preacher!

ॐ ॐ ॐ

40 • ". . . He restores my soul."
— *Psalm 23:3a (NIV)*

41 • Say thank you often!

42 • God has something to say to you. You can hear Him if you listen. — *Bob Benson*

❧❧❧

43 · Always keep your head up,
but be careful to keep your
nose on a friendly level.

❧❧❧

44 · Distribute your outline to the congregation and watch them take notes.

45 · Don't let yesterday take up too much of today.
  – *Will Rogers*

46 · Successful churches are seeker sensitive.

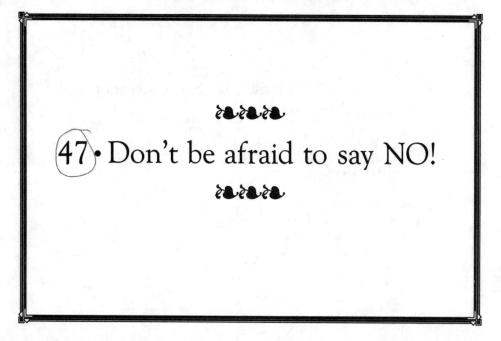

47 · Don't be afraid to say NO!

(48) · Words can never adequately convey the incredible impact of our attitude toward life. The longer I live, the more convinced I become that life is 10% what happens to us and 90% how we respond to it. – *Charles Swindoll*

49 · Leadership is influence! – *John Maxwell*

50 · Read biographies – not just fiction.

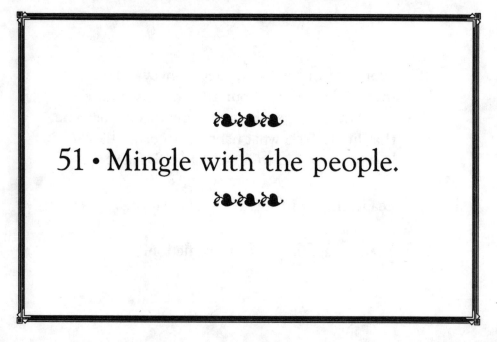

51 · Mingle with the people.

52 • Drink 8 glasses of water per day.

53 • Be a good tipper, not a tightwad.

54 • Commitment: another name for successful ministry.

ই&ই&ই&

55 · Surround yourself with a
strong staff that is diverse
in ability qualifications.

ই&ই&ই&

(56) • Preach the Word in the power of the Holy Spirit.

57 • Never ask a child to explain a prayer request during services.

ᓎ ᓎ ᓎ

(58) · Reverse the divorce rate; marry only people who will accept pre-marital counseling.

ᓎ ᓎ ᓎ

59 · The last lesson we learn is "hands off" that God's hands may be on.

60 · Never go into business with members of your church.

61 · The greatest use of life is to spend it for something that will outlast it.

62 · Worship is man's answer
to God's call.

63 • Vision: the ability to see beyond the obvious.

64 • Learn how to accept a gift from a lay person;
they need fulfillment in giving too!
– *Jim Van Hook*

65 • When you affirm big, believe big, and pray big,
big things happen. – *Norman Vincent Peale*

ஃஃஃ

66 · Make the local church as close as the street.
– *Tom Wallace*

ஃஃஃ

67 · Never ask for a clergy discount!

68 · Get to know what it is you don't know as fast as you can. – *Robert Heller*

69 · Always go last in line.

ৡৡৡ

70 · There are two sides to
every argument . . .
until you take one.

ৡৡৡ

71 • Evangelism cannot be an optional plan of the local church; it must become its highest priority.

72 • Have a pew registry — you'll find lots of prospects.

73 · Be yourself in the pulpit.

74 · Let the congregation laugh at your mistakes publicly . . . they will anyhow!

75 · The school of affliction graduates rare scholars.
  – *Eleanor Doan*

76 · Membership in a civic organization reaps huge dividends!

ॐॐॐ

77 · Remember Secretary's Day!

ॐॐॐ

78 · Return your phone calls promptly!

79 · Drink only one cup of coffee per day.

80 · The church board must function as a board of directors, not as a large committee.

ഀഀഀ

81 · "Cast all your anxiety on him because he cares for you." – *1 Peter 5:7*

ഀഀഀ

82 · "Tonight I am speaking free of charge . . . and I think you'll agree, I'm worth every penny of it!"

83 · A sharp tongue and a dull mind are usually found in the same head.

84 · Ministry in its purest and simplist form is love . . . Ministry is, in fact, doing love! – *Win Arn*

❧❧❧

85 · Ideas are funny little
things . . . they won't
work unless you do.

❧❧❧

86 · The greatness of a man is determined not by what it takes to get him going . . . but by what it takes to stop him.

87 · Never answer a letter while you are angry.

88 · Faith doesn't demand miracles . . . it accomplishes them. – *Robert Schuller*

89 · Be your own critic . . .
listen to last Sunday's
sermon on tape.

90 · Success comes in "cans" — failures come in "can'ts" – *Robert Schuller*

91 · Whenever things sound easy, it turns out there's one part you didn't hear.

92 · Make sure that the principles you believe should guide your organization are clear to you and to others.
– *James M. Kouzes and Barry Z. Posner*

93 · Write out your message in
full occasionally. It's a
great exercise!

94 · Remember the people who have helped you on your path to success in the ministry.

95 · Never allow the salary to determine your acceptance of a church.

96 · I can do plenty alone . . . but with God, I can do more! – *Ken Taylor*

ঌঌঌ

97 · Pay your bills on time!

ঌঌঌ

98 · Cut the fat in your diet.

99 · Never handle church money.

100 · It is the trial of our faith that makes us healthy
in God's sight. – *Oswald Chambers*

❧❧❧

101 · The Holy Spirit is the author of dreams.
– *H. B. London*

❧❧❧

102 • Put cartoons in your church board reports. It'll lighten up the place.

103 • An idea is more than information; it is information with legs that is headed somewhere.

104 • A smile is a gently curved line that sets a lot of things straight.

ája ája ája

105 · God will not look you
over for medals, degrees,
or diplomas — but for
scars.

ája ája ája

106 · Be prepared for any answer when asking a
female patient for an explanation as to why she
is in the hospital.

107 · Short notes make a lasting impression.

108 · "May the words of my mouth and the
meditation of my heart be pleasing in your
sight, O Lord, my Rock and my Redeemer."
– *Psalm 19:14 (NIV)*

એએએ

(109)· Send thank you notes
for every act of kindness.

એએએ

110 · Give books and tapes for gifts. They make a permanent impression.

111 · After the ship has sunk, everyone knows how she might have been saved.

112 · If the structure or systems of the organization cause people to feel unvalued, unworthy, or unwise, they will look for ways to beat the system. – *William J. Schwarz*

113 · Be quick to ask for forgiveness.

114· "Trust in the Lord with all your heart and lean not on your own understanding; in all your ways acknowledge him, and he will make your paths straight." — *Proverbs 3:5-6 (NIV)*

115· We kneel, how weak! We rise, how full of power.

116· Wear flip-flops in the shower at health centers!

117 · Instead of making resignations every Monday, wait until Tuesday one week.

118 • Practice the attitude of gratitude.
    – *Norman Vincent Peale*

119 • A good book contains more real wealth than a
    good bank. – *Roy L. Smith*

120 • " ' . . . For I know the plans I have for you,'
    declares the Lord, 'plans to prosper you and
    not harm you, plans to give you hope and a
    future. . . ' " – *Jeremiah 29:11 (NIV)*

ᏰᏰᏰ

121 · Go vote! Bad officials are
the ones elected by good
citizens who do not vote.
– *George Bush*

ᏰᏰᏰ

122 · Keep only reference books and any book of spiritual content. Sell old books and use the money to buy new ones!

123 · I am always ready to learn, although I do not always like being taught. – *Winston Churchill*

124 · Write out your goals.

ఌఌఌ

125 · Keep your enemies up close where you can see them.

ఌఌఌ

126 • The test of good manners is being able to put up with bad ones. – *Maurice Seitler*

127 • Always be kind to your predecessor; you'll be one someday!

128 • Readers are leaders! – *Warren Bennis*

❧❧❧

129· Remove Christ from
Christianity and you
have just an empty shell.
– *Josh McDowell*

❧❧❧

130 · Commend more than you criticize!

131 · Discipline your children in private. Public discipline will cause future resentment.

132 · He listens well who takes notes.
— *Dante Alighieri*

❧❧❧

133 · If you are on time,
you are late.

❧❧❧

134 · You shouldn't criticize your wife's judgement; look who she married.

135 · Exercise 15 minutes a day 5 times per week.

136 · Genius is one percent inspiration and ninety-nine percent perspiration. – *Thomas Edison*

ཏེ་ཏེ་ཏེ་

137 · Few sinners are saved
after the first twenty
minutes of a sermon.
– *Mark Twain*

ཏེ་ཏེ་ཏེ་

138 · You don't get two chances to make a good first impression.

139 · Read local papers daily.

140 · Let your walk match your talk!

❧❧❧

(141) • Use an illustration or
humor every five minutes
in your message.

❧❧❧

142 • Some people have greatness thrust upon them. Very few have excellence thrust upon them . . . they achieve it. – *John Gardner*

143 • Pray shorter prayers in public . . . have your devotions at home.

144 • Perfect freedom through perfect obedience. – *E. Stanley Jones*

145 · If you fail to plan, you are unknowingly planning to fail.

146 · Plan your work and work your plans!

147 · If you fail to plan, you are unknowingly planning to fail.

148 · Anointing and authority come from God, not from ability, education and experience.

149 · Never drive the church
bus!

150 • If you think you're a total failure, remember
this: Your greatest success . . . will forever
remain . . . God's secret!

151 • Never look at what you have lost . . . look at
what you have left.

152 • "Test everything. Hold on to the good."
– *I Thessalonians 5:21*

153 · Your attitude is the key
to your success in the
ministry. — *John Maxwell*

154 · Ask God to give you tears. A compassionate heart from the pulpit will touch others.

155 · Involve the laity in pastoral care . . . you'll live longer and they'll be happier.

156 · Character is long-standing habit. – *Plutarch*

ੴ ੴ ੴ

157 · God demands our
tithes and deserves
our offerings.
– *Stephen Olford*

ੴ ੴ ੴ

158 · Vision always precedes victory.

159 · "One of life's most painful moments comes when we must admit that we didn't do our homework, that we are not prepared."
– *NFL football broadcaster, Merlin Olsen*

160 · A minute of thought is worth an hour of talk.
– *William James*

❧❧❧

161 · Return phone calls
at the end of each hour.

❧❧❧

162 · Be sure your brain is in gear before opening your mouth.

163 · Remind church ushers that they are your hand extended.

164 · *Anger* is just one letter short of *Danger*.

૨ટ૨ટ૨ટ

165 · Procrastination is opportunity's natural assasin. – *Victor Kiam*

૨ટ૨ટ૨ટ

166 · Leave the church slowly, greet your church
neighbors warmly, extend your hand quickly
to visitors and take the Lord home with you!
– *Paul Martin*

167 · Instead of ordering a banana split, order just a
banana and save a zillion fats and calories.

168 · Faults are the easiest things to find.

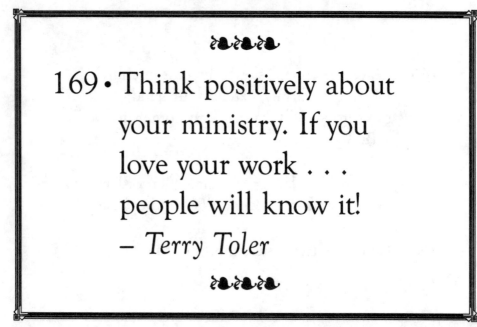

169 · Think positively about
your ministry. If you
love your work . . .
people will know it!
– *Terry Toler*

170 · Go to community sporting events. You'll get to see a different side of your congregation members and it's great P.R.!

171 · If I had only three years to serve the Lord, I would spend two of them studying and preparing. – *Donald Grey Barnhouse*

172 · Counting time is not so important as making time count.

❧❧❧

173 · If your mind goes blank,
don't forget to turn off
the sound.

❧❧❧

174 · Don't practice elevator evangelism. You win people to Christ through your influence.

175 · Reaching high keeps a man on his toes.

176 · God will either lighten our load or strengthen our backs.

177 · Don't count the days —
make the days count.

178 · The best preparation for tomorrow is the proper use of today.

179 · Even if you're on the right track, you'll get run over if you just sit there.

180 · Those who do not know how to weep with their whole heart don't know how to laugh either. – *Golda Meir*

ھﻻﻻﻻ

181 · Make your children's
special days and events
standing appointments.

ھﻻﻻﻻ

182 · Live each day as if it is your last; some day you will be right.

183 · What a world this would be if we could forget our troubles as easily as we forget our blessings.

184 · Success is not a destination . . . it is a road.

185 · Never sign church
documents.

186 · An upright man can never be a downright failure.

187 · "Blessed are the peacemakers, for they will be called sons of God." – *Matthew 5:9 (NIV)*

188 · A smile adds a great deal to face value.

❧❧❧

189 · "But God demonstrates his own love for us in this: While we were still sinners, Christ died for us." – *Romans 5:8 (NIV)*

❧❧❧

190 · Keep breath mints in your suit pocket.

191 · Never learn how to run the church copy machine.

192 · Kindness is a hard thing to give away — it usually comes back.

193 · . . . Man cannot find the true essential joy of his life anywhere but in his relationship to God.

– *Oswald Chambers*

194 · Cut fat and cholesterol by reading labels.

195 · A church committee is the only life form with twelve stomachs and no brain.

196 · For penance, play 15 holes of golf instead of 18 holes.

197 · Don't worship your work
. . . worship God!

198 · Never use position for financial gain.

199 · A smile costs nothing but creates much.

200 · Keep Saturday evenings for study and
meditation. You'll preach better on Sunday!

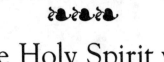

201 · The Holy Spirit within
is the secret, the center,
and the source of my
power and poise.
– *E. Stanley Jones*

202 · If you think you know what's going on, I can almost guarantee that you are hopelessly confused. – *Joe T. Ford*

203 · Don't use your preaching voice in every day conversations.

204 · A train of thought is not always on time.

205 · Share the ministry
with others!

206 · Reading is to the mind what exercise is to the body.

207 · Avoid off-color jokes . . . especially about the Lord.

208 · A powerless pastor is a prayerless pastor.

209 · Happiness is the perfume that you cannot pour on others without getting a few drops on yourself.

210 · Joy is not happiness; joy is the result of the perfect fulfillment of the purpose of life.

211 · Try the garlic diet; you won't lose weight but you will look slimmer from a distance.

212 · Well done is better than well said.
– *Ben Franklin*

213 · Raise your voice occasionally when you preach. There's nothing worse than a monotone.

214 · Never match new converts with legalistic parishioners.

215 · "We are all here for a spell . . . get all the good laughs you can." – *Will Rogers*

216 · Humility is the hallmark of holiness.

217 · Prayer is need finding
a voice.
– *Ralph A. Herring*

218 · Pay attention to the parking lot greeters
— they will give forth the first impression
of the pastor.

219 · I am resolved never to do anything which I
should be afraid to do if it were the last hour
of my life. – *Jonathan Edwards*

220 · Never betray a confidence!

221 · Example is not the main thing in influencing others. It is the only thing. – *Albert Schweitzer*

222 · Care for the poor . . . God will bless your faithfulness!

223 · The meaning of sacrifice is the deliberate giving of the best I have to God that we may make it His and mine forever; if I cling to it, I lose it, and so does God. – *Oswald Chambers*

224 · Experience is yesterday's answer to today's problems.

225 · A new necktie makes an old suit look new!

226 · Real leaders are ordinary people with extra-ordinary determination.

227 · A camel is a horse put together by a church committee.

228 · Hire people who are as strong as yourself.

229 · You cannot effectively lead others until you can manage yourself!

230 · Empower those who are gifted in areas where you are weak.

231 · Most people commit suicide with a fork rather than with a gun.

232 · If you ask for a dollar, you must be willing to give a dollar. The leader must model giving.
– *Melvin Maxwell*

233 · Trust, not authority, is the pathway to results in teams. – *Gerry S. Howe*

234 • Take time to go to your kids' ball games.
They'll love you for it later!

235 • Above all, focus on speed in making decisions:
quality will be the consequence.

236 • Don't miss many Sundays . . . you must be
present to win! – *David Vaughn*

237 · One of the best ways to get on your feet is to first get on your knees.

238 • By being proactive with your people when initiating change, you can avoid toxic behaviors that kill productivity. – *Millard N. Macadam*

239 • Use a handkerchief with each baptismal candidate. It will keep water out of their nose and keep you from a panic-attacked parishioner.

240 • Give away tapes when you are finished with them.

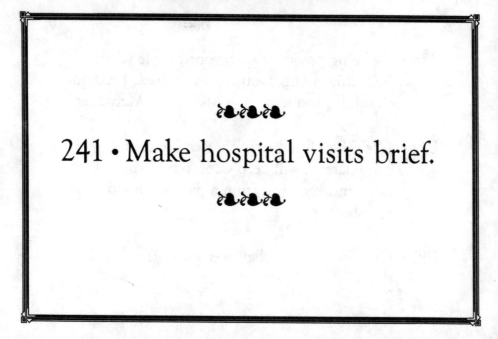

241 · Make hospital visits brief.

242 · Leaders need to spend less time in the present and more time inhabiting the future.
– *Ellen R. Hart*

243 · Rewarding employees for exceptional work is critical to keeping them motivated to do their best. – *Ken Blanchard*

244 · Always give an invitation at baptism – it's a great time to win new converts!

245 · ". . . Everyone should be quick to listen, slow to speak and slow to become angry. . ."
– *James 1:19 (NIV)*

246 · It is important to see the difference between leadership and management. Some institutions are well-managed but poorly led. That is a mating that begets mediocrity.
– *William A. Marstele*

247 · Never be afraid to get your hands dirty.

248 · Zeal without knowledge is a runaway horse.

249 · The fewer the words
the better the prayer.

– *Martin Luther*

250 · Work for the Lord. The pay isn't much but His retirement plan is out of this world.

251 · Promote the bad days and let the good ones take care of themselves. – *John Maxwell*

252 · Growl all day and you'll feel dog tired at night.

253 · The person who rows the boat generally doesn't have time to rock it.

254 · I'd rather be a failure at something I enjoy
than be a success at something I hate.
– *George Burns*

255 · Treat your office staff like a million!

256 · Sight sees that which is visible and present,
vision sees that which is invisible and yet to
be. – *Michael Hodgin*

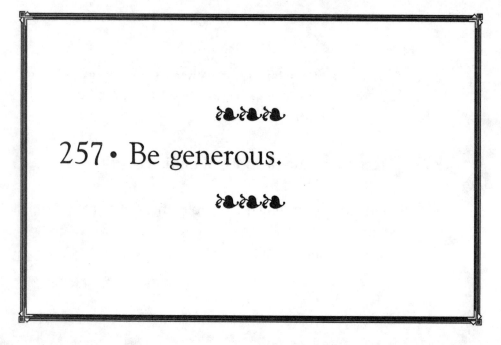

257 · Be generous.

258 · Profit is not a value, it is a measure or a result, not a belief or an attitude.

259 · Plan to be 5 minutes early to all appointments.

260 · Wear a white linen square in your coat pocket. It'll dress up your suit!

261 · When I am wrong, dear Lord, make me easy to change, and when I am right, make me easy to live with. – *Peter Marshall*

262 · Steady progress made in tiny steps gets us
there eventually. . ."
– *Alan Skelton and William C. Miller*

263 · Accomplishment is ability stripped of doubt.

264 · I hear, and I forget. I see, and I remember. I
do, and I understand. – *Ancient sanskrit*

265 · Life holds nothing within it which Christ has not conquered.
– *E. Stanley Jones*

266 · Parents who are afraid to put their foot down
have children who step on their toes.

267 · "Where there is no revelation, the people cast
off restraint; but blessed is he who keeps the
law." – *Proverbs 29:18 (NIV)*

268 · It is better to say "thank you" and not mean it
than to mean it and not say it.

269 · The happiness of your life
depends on the quality
of your thoughts.

270 · Always expect the best out of people and you'll
get the best!

271 · God never asks about our ability or inability
— just about our availability.

272 · Simplify your message
so that an eight-year-old
can understand.

273 • The true art of memory is the art of attention.

274 • You cannot do a kindness too soon because you never know how soon it will be too late.
– *Ralph Waldo Emerson*

275 • While faith makes all things possible, it is love that makes all things easy. – *Evan H. Hopkins*

276 · Say I love you to your
wife and kids when
you sign off from
a phone call.

277 • Purdue University researchers tracked 300 children and their parents for 14 years and concluded that "dads are as important as moms to the emotional health and adjustments of their kids."
– *Men's Health Magazine*

278 • The best mirror is an old friend.

279 • The school of affliction graduates rare scholars. – *Eleanor Doan*

❧❧❧

280 · A good laugh is sunshine in the house.

❧❧❧

281 · Friendship is like a bank account. You can't continue to draw on it without making deposits.

282 · A true friend walks in when the rest of the world walks out.

283 · If I had kept my mouth shut, I wouldn't be here — the sign under a mounted fish.

284 · Never use an illustration about your family in a sermon without their permission.

285 · "Those who sow in tears will reap with songs of joy. He who goes out weeping, carrying seed to sow, will return with songs of joy, carrying sheaves with him." – *Psalm 126:5-6 (NIV)*

286 · Send flowers to your spouse with no apparent reason in mind!

287 · Block study time, family time, and recreational time on your weekly calendar.

288 · It may be difficult to wait on the Lord, but it's worse to wish you had.

289 · When you must choose between a late night in the office or going home. . . go home!

290 · If I do not forgive, then I break the bridge — forgiveness — over which I too must pass.

291 · Believe the best about people, and if you're wrong, you've only made a mistake on the side of love. – *Melvin Maxwell*

292 · People don't care how much you know until they know how much you care. – *John Maxwell*

293 · One individual life may be of priceless value to God's purposes, and yours may be that life.
– *Kathleen M. Chambers*

294 · There are many good preachers; but, the more hands you shake, the better preacher you'll become.

295 · Rid yourself of a negative mindset unless you want people to avoid you.

296 · While serving, you are being trained for greater responsibility.

297 · When a prayer concern is given . . . pray instantly!

298 · Don't change your hairstyle suddenly.

299 · "Now to him who is able to do immeasurably more than all we ask or imagine, according to his power that is at work within us, to him be glory in the church and in Christ Jesus throughout all generations, for ever and ever! Amen." – *Ephesians 3:20-21*

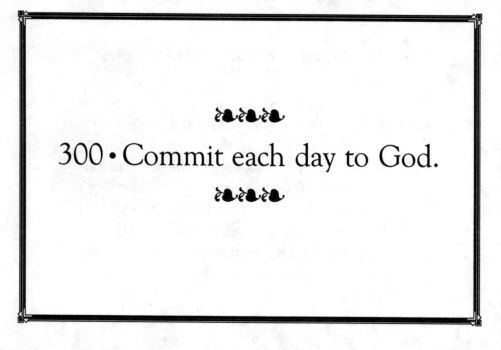

300 · Commit each day to God.

Stan Toler presently serves as Vice President for INJOY Ministries as well as Pastor-In-Residence at Southern Nazarene University in Bethany, Oklahoma. His experience ranges from twenty-five-plus years of pastoring, teaching, and speaking on subjects of evangelism and church growth. Stan has published works on  topics such as soulwinning, church management, and leadership and has videos available on vision planning and stewardship. Hundreds of pastors have been encouraged by Stan's genuine love and concern for others which has initially made him known as a "Pastor to Pastors."

Additional copies of this book are available
from your local bookstore.

P. O. Box 55388
Tulsa, OK 74155